this book belongs to:

____

The KKandbabyj Family

KKandbabyJ

Keren & Khoa

Keren and Khoa

Jackson

Jackson

Landon

landon and raccoonies

Sutton

Sutton and Foxy

kids meeting Moro

landon Caying on Moro

Sutton holding Meeko

First Fish

Sutton Moro Foxy

Super Landon

Jackson Landon Dancing

Jackson landon Sword Fight

Um, Khoa! Landon found a mouse outside!
Can I keep him?!?

landon's New Pet

Wedding

Keren Meeko

Apple
Cider
Vinegar

YouTube Challenge

Paddleboard Push

Khoa & Jackson Surfing

Landon's Haircut

Landon Sleeping

Snorkeling Kids

Khoa throwing Jackson

Yonie Landon

Come on Nay Nay, we need more sand!
I'm going as fast as I can!

Kids Diggin on the Beach

Moro's first Puppuccino

Jackson Landon Lemonade

Sutton playing with his car

Sutton Narwhal

Sutton is a
dragon!

Sutton is a Dragon

landon and a box

Illustrator
Sara McClanahan